Zoo Map

Written by Sheila May Bird
Illustrated by AndoTwin

Contents

At the Zoo

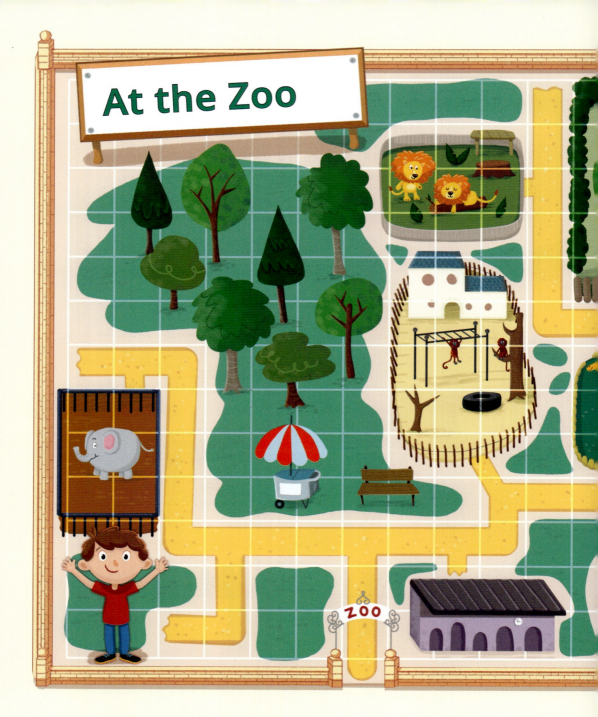

This is a map of the zoo.
You need it to find your way around.

Lines split this map into little squares.
North is at the top of the map.

Getting Around

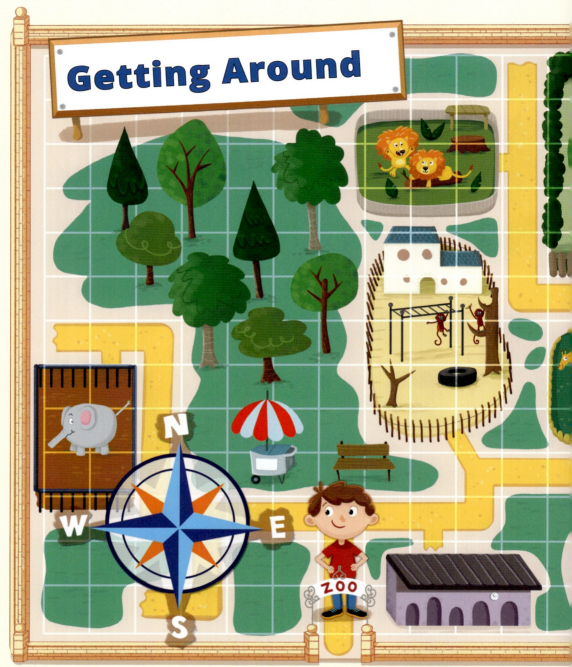

This is a compass.
A compass has four points:
North, East, South and West.

You can use the compass to follow
the squares and find things.
Can you see where you are on the map?

Let's Go!

You are here

ZOO

You are by the gate.
Let's use this map to find some animals.

Go three squares East and one square
North. Which animal have you found?

The Tamarin

It's a tamarin.
A tamarin is a small monkey with
a long tail. It jumps high up in the trees.

Now go six squares East and one square North. Which animal will you find next?

The Anteater

You have found an anteater.
Anteaters have a long tongue but no teeth.
They can eat 35 thousand ants a day!

Go one square West and five squares North to find the next animal.

The Toucan

This is a toucan.
It is a bird with a very long beak.
Toucans nest in tree holes.

Next, go five squares East and three squares South. What is hiding in the cave?

The Komodo Dragon

It's a Komodo dragon.
The Komodo dragon is a very big lizard.
Look out, it eats anything meaty!

14

Last stop! Go one square West and five squares South. Can you see where you are going? Hooray! It's the toy shop!

Index